SACRED SYMBOLS
OF
HINDUISM

SACRED SYMBOLS
OF
HINDUISM

J.R. SANTIAGO

BOOK FAITH INDIA
Delhi

SACRED SYMBOLS OF HINDUISM

Published by
BOOK FAITH INDIA
414-416 Express Tower
Azadpur Commercial Complex
Delhi, India 110033
Tel. [91-11] 713-2459. Fax [91-11] 724-9674
E-mail: pilgrim@del2.vsnl.net.in

Distributed by
PILGRIMS BOOK HOUSE
P.O.Box 3872
Kathmandu, Nepal
Tel. [977-1] 424942. Fax [977-1] 424943.
E-mail: pilgrims@wlink.com.np
WebSite: pilgrimsbooks.com

Varanasi Branch
PILGRIMS BOOK HOUSE
B 27/98-A-8, Durga Kund
Varanasi, India 221001
Tel. [91-542] 314060. Fax [91-542] 314059, 312788
E-mail: pilgrim@lw1.vsnl.net.in

Artwork and Text design by Dr. Sasya
Layout by Naresh Subba

1st Edition
Copyright © 1999 Book Faith India

ISBN 81-7303-181-9

Printed in India

CONTENTS

Preface

Worship is a symbol of spiritualism. It represents a belief in an unseen power, the Underlying Principle of the phenomenal universe and life. This endows life with a profound meaning and with the intuitive notion that life extends beyond the physical into the spiritual.

The pulse beat of life from the beginning to the end is worship. It is no longer just surviving but worshipping and this is living. The spiritual aspect of life is not set aside, but attended with reverence, side by side with physical existence.

In worship, illumination dawns and the spiritual becomes more important than the physical aspect of life. Icons are made and temples are erected to house them, all symbols of the emerging spiritualism. More symbols and ritual artefacts are made to transmute into simple understandable abstract concepts.

The symbols are essential and have practical applications. The abstract becomes the obvious and there arises a deeper understanding of the mystery of life. There is more reverence, worship becomes a way of life.

The symbolism of Hinduism, although exoteric and esoteric, is the key to understanding. Not only of the spiritual creed of India but of the mystery of human existence and the spiritual urge or impulse in man. It represents the doctrine that spirit is inherent in man.

It is hoped that this short introductory work on Hindu symbolism, though not exhaustive, will help determine if the doctrine is valid.

Foreword

Hinduism is of course no longer an unknown creed, and its symbolism is no longer completely esoteric, for it has spread throughout the whole world during this century.

The symbols are no longer esoteric, but they remain only superficially known, with their real meaning or philosophical basis remaining obscure to most people. Even the significance of the most common symbols, like the swastika or the OM, is hardly known.

Symbolism simplifies abstract concepts. They convey their meanings by intelligible forms in the cultural milieu from which they have evolved and developed. Symbols remain numerous and essential in the practice of external worship. Not until worshippers have become enlightened will the symbols and external form of worship disappears, to be replaced by 'Inner Worship.'

The spiritual symbols are a reminder of the Transcendental Essence, which represents the eternal aspects of human existence, and therefore are reassuring in a similar manner as the Cross is in Christendom.

It is basically polymourphous monotheism. The innumerable attributes of the Absolute has made Hinduism pantheistic. It is a product of the syncretism of the aboriginal sacrificial offerings and the Aryan Vedic ritual worship.

It is not merely because their beginnings are lost in the mists of primeval time that they arrive in our time, primitive, mysterious and mystical, but because they have emerged and evolved in an entirely different environment and different concepts from those of other creeds that have cropped out of other cultural matrix.

In this short general introductory work on the sacred symbols of Hinduism, an attempt has been made to present their meaning and significance in an exhaustive but comprehensive manner. However, this is simply impossible to achieve in this small volume.

Of the really important symbols, the more common or ubiquitous, though abstract or mystical, have been given in-depth treatment to make them understandable. The rest, also abstruse in concept, but essential as accessories, have been explained briefly for a quick grasp of their significance. The importance of these symbols, to one encountering them for the first time, is whether under concentrated scrutiny the fundamentals of Hinduism will stand valid when compared with any other established creed.

INTRODUCTION

On the whole the intellectual impression that Hinduism presents is that it has sprung out of the Vedic Age. But the evolution of Hinduism started long before the beginning of the Vedic Age.

From the investigation of subcontinental archaeology, the linguistic studies, and the study of folk art forms — usually inspired by religion – emerges evidence of native animism, fetishism, and primitive mysticism. These must have evolved out of the native experience and observations of nature.

With fear and insecurity in their surroundings, feeling that they were at the mercy of incomprehensible primal forces, people learned to placate, appease and propitiate them. Fear was the primal impulse to worship. This was the original conception of religion. Then began the worship of 'sacred' trees, rocks, caves, and habitats of the supernatural, like the fairies, who became divinities of forests, hills, caves and rivers.

They may have observed them to be beneficient, quiescent, but occasionally wrathful. It can certainly be asserted that it may have occurred to the primitive mind to appease or propitiate these supernatural forces. The natural elements and beasts they discovered possessed power and other attributes, the meanings of which were expanded until they acquired mystical significance.

Prayers – the origin of mantras — were developed, with charms invented with magic designs, probably the prototype of mandalas. The oldest apparently was the triangle, symbol of the Goddess of Fertility, found in caves and ruins of prehistoric settlements.

Over the millenia a plethora of symbols of their rituals proliferated. From the elementary and primitive to the complex, abstruse and sophisticated. These were endowed with the essence of mysticism. The worship that evolved was Tantra, a mystical discipline, which antedates the Vedic Age. Thus, almost all the sacred symbols are non-Vedic.

It cannot precisely be defined as aboriginal or non-Aryan, for there has been no study of the racial configuration in the subcontinent of the earliest time when worship evolved and developed. It is possible that the first batch of a small wandering pastoral Aryan tribe may have arrived, and by interbreeding with the aborigines, completely disappeared as a distinct racial group; but it is also possible that interbreeding gave impetus to the intellectual fermentation that eventually made them have sharper and deeper insights, and thus sophisticated in their overview of the supernatural forces in their environment.

They worshipped a variety of divinities; the sun, the sky, the moon, the fire, and even the beasts, even the mysterious reproductive or generative part of the human body, and perhaps also dynamic tribal leaders who became legendary and there arose a polytheistic pantheon of gods and goddesses.

They later divined, however, that there was only one Absolute Power, the Mother Goddess with millions of attributes, her emanations or transcendental manifestations in the phenomenal world. It was thus fundamentally monotheistic. The worship of the Mother Goddess is Tantric, which subordinates the Gods, who are only manifestations of her attributes and supreme power. She is everything.

With the arrival of the Vedic Age, the creed of the indigenous aborigines fused with that of the new Aryan tribes who arrived later. It is noteworthy that the Vedic Age took the whole indigenous system of worship, along with the deities and ritual artefacts, practically unchanged.

On the whole, indigenous symbology remained unaltered, with perhaps the underlying philosophy, complicated and abstract, undergoing some modification and improvement. The only great changes were in the transformation of superiority from female to male deities. In the masculinisation of the deities by the chauvinistic Aryan, they also acquired the symbols, attributes or qualities of the female deities. In spite of this effort to relegate the goddesses to an inferior position, the instinctive or intuitive propensity is to worship the Mother Goddess.

The symbolism of Hinduism arrives in our time amazingly primitive yet complex, abstract, even intricately designed and conceived, and therefore almost incomprehensible. Simple objects, invested with qualities unseen on the surface, do not give up their secrets with just a cursory or perfunctory interest shown in them. They have all been imbued with metaphysical masks exhibiting only the outward reality, the illusion, but hiding the inner reality.

The reality, inherent in the illusion, finally bursts, and the simple concept emerges, abstract but whole and complete. The mystery is resolved. The only endeavour left is to experience its essence — the vitality of the concept in the human heart.

When a deeper curiosity focuses on it, like the lotus bud it bursts open into a beautiful flower. The whole Hindu world of phenomena becomes more intelligible. Modern day scientists claim that the original primal sound frequency of the Big Bang is still reverberating in the cosmos. And this is the OM mantra that is still resonating in the womb of the Mother Goddess.

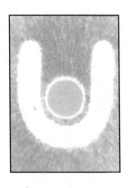

I

HINDUISM

Hinduism is essentially nature worship. Man stands in awe of its beneficence, beauty and power. As discernment dawns, he is delighted and becomes joyous in his discovery. What lies hidden but paramount in his heart is the Mother Goddess.

Nature, as mother, provides everything for the sustenance of life. There is absolute harmony between man and nature. And there is sonorous peace in the land, with man's soul glowing with the rising of the sun and becoming quiescent with its setting in the evening. At night he folds his hands in pranam to the scintillating beauty of chandra, the moon, which in its crescent shape mesmerizes him. He does pranam to all nature, in all four directions, giving thanks for the benedictions received for that day. In the bosom of nature he feels secure and contented.

From the moment he wakes up, to the time he retires, it is worship all day. His creed is a way of life. All his life. In the end he turns inward into himself, to realize the Mother Goddess in his heart.

Symbols As Sacred Art

The symbols presented here practically have their origin in Tantra and are therefore Tantric art, intended to evoke a higher level of perception. Its real significance lies, not in its aesthetic value, but in the philosophy of life it displays.

'Tantric art is visual metaphysics.' It is a synthesis of the outer and inner worlds. The psychophysical unity, man's link with the cosmos, is a reality.

The symbols are allegorical, a product of creative psychic manifestations, with meaning hidden in their enigmatic metaphysical undertones. It is in this symbolism that the real is made visible; it becomes a dynamic visual aid for self-enlightenment.

The symbols are ageless; they survive from age to age, through generations. They have a timeless quality, representing the governing principles of life. Tantric art emanates from ignorance: it is to realize what is intuitively known. The physical world is the workshop in which to realize this inner reality for a deep sense of fulfillment – enlightenment.

This is its ultimate purpose.

II

METAPHYSICAL SYMBOLS

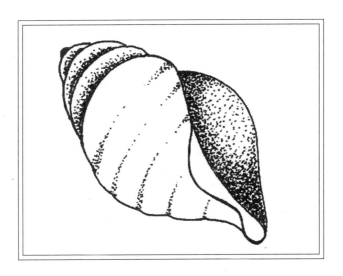

The metaphysical philosophical symbols of religion began with a very simple concept, but with hidden mystical significance. Whatever sophistication it acquired later also contained the hidden essence of the Absolute.

Over the millennia this is a concept which never suffered any change, in spite of the numerous philosophical treatises or religious ideologies that developed and were scattered all over the spiritual landscape of the subcontinent.

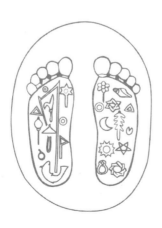

TANTRA

      Tantra is presented here as an extremely important doctrine, for in it are the   philosophy and principles involved in the attainment of enlightenment. In this brief introductory work it contains, to some extent, the whole concept of Hinduism, as it has evolved and developed.

      Tantra is pre-Vedic. It represents one of the earliest forms of worship of the Mother Goddess, whose original symbol is the upright triangle, which represented fecundity. The female principle was later represented by the inverted triangle, and it is what is actually worshipped as existing in the Sri Chakra, also known as Sri Yantra.

      'Tan' means to expand and 'tra' to protect. It is to protect expansion of self-awareness.

      It expounds a mystical philosophy and the principles to be followed to attain enlightenment. It does not renounce worldly life, nor practice asceticism, but makes use of human impulses and energy, with apparent detachment. Tantric practices culminate in a state of mind totally independent of the bonds of human existence. It makes use of the Triguya – the three mysteries or forces: the spirit, the speech, and the body. All three forces are focused on enlightenment.

      The spirit is represented by the yantra which is originally a mandala; the speech by the mantra; and the body by the yoga asanas, physical exercises; all methods of awakening latent forces in the human body.

The yantra and the mantra — as in the Sri Chakra — are concerned mainly with the integrated structure of the universe and its fundamental unity, sustained by the power of the Mother Goddess. This fundamental principle applies to the microcosm — the individual — as well.

Tantra is concerned mainly with the body, the microcosm. It holds that the individual contains within himself all the essential dimensions of the cosmos, and that the universe unfolds itself in the development of the individual.

The universe though represents separation, diffusion, expansion, but the individual represents focussing and compactness. The principle and power of the Mother Goddess can be discerned more clearly at the microcosmic than at the macrocosmic level.

The tantric supreme divinity is the Mother Goddess, and its basic philosophical principle is found in the Sri Chakra, in which the union of Shiva (male) and Shakti (female) principles is fundamental. It works in the main on the human body, its physical constitution along with the subtle body which is said to have centers of energy known as chakras.

The study of chakras is very complex and involves exercises — yoga asanas — and mantras, and finally meditation . Its goal is to awaken the kundalini also known as Shakti, the female principle coiled at the bottom of the spinal column, and make it rise to join Shiva, the male principle, at the crown of the head.

When union occurs or is successful a mystical event takes place - and there is self-realisation.

MANTRA

ॐ
देवकीनन्दनाय विद्महे,
वासुदेवाय धीमहि।
तन्नो कृष्ण:प्रचोदयात्॥

Mantras are words of power, usually a combination of Sanskrit syllables used as invocations. They are prayers, either articulated loudly with proper sound and rhythm or chanted repeatedly.

A name is a symbol of an attribute or of the reality it signifies or represents. A divine name is not just a label, but a sacred form, which when repeated over and over again, establishes a rapport between the deity and the devotee.

There is power and dynamism in the mantra, which must be uttered with proper attention to rhythm and sound to establish resonance. Some mantras are to be uttered mentally, quietly, and most particularly the sacred OM mantra.

'Man' means the soul or mind, and 'tra' to protect or guide. Thus it is the guide of the soul or protector of the mind. Mantras like OM also assist in awakening the spiritual forces in the devotee.

OM

In the beginning out of the void — *sunyata* — sprang this triliteral sacred syllable. It sounds like the Genesis: 'In the beginning was the Word...'

It is regarded as the primal sound which reverberated in the creation of the universe. It is therefore considered the holiest and most powerful mantra, and is known as *Paramatma* or God. Being the supreme mantra, it must precede all other mantras, otherwise the latter won't have the power or the presence of the divine power.

Its articulation must precede any work undertaken, for it stands at the beginning of creation, its nurturing, preservation, and its absorption, not dissolution. This corresponds to the three elements — *gunas* – created by the Big Bang: the spirit-mind-body representing the Hindu trinity of Brahma-Vishnu-Shiva. It must be uttered with the utmost care, or otherwise it must be articulated mentally, quietly with reverence. In religious rituals, however, it is chanted. Its sound is the focus of meditation.

It is usually written as OM. The actual mystic syllable is A-U-M heard in a deep meditative state. It pervades and permeates the whole cosmos; it is inherent in life and is linked with human procreation. It is the Mother Goddess' manifesting symbol.

When uttered, it purifies and activates certain forces in the human body and helps transcend worldly problems. It is regarded to have existed before and after creation. It is imperishable, and therefore the symbol of the infinite. It resides and is present in Silence, and represents the entire manifested and unmanifested world.

MANDALA

Among the Hindus, a mandala simply means a circle — which has a universal mystical significance. It is a symbolic graphic diagram invested with the spirit of a deity. When finished it becomes a yantra — a ritual artefact — an object of worship, a meditation device for concentration, for the purpose of attaining real spiritual insights, and of activating supernatural forces in the human body.

The process in preparing a mandala involves the gathering and concentration in a diagrammatic design of the important aspects of the worshipper's world, his own psychological constitution, and for these two dynamic forces to interact. It is therefore a focusing of energies for their effective play or interaction. Its function is to protect, create, integrate and transform.

The center, a dot, is the origin of a mandala. It is a symbol apparently free of dimensions. It means a 'seed,' 'sperm,' 'drop,' the salient starting point. It is the gathering center in which the outside energies are drawn, and in the act of drawing the forces, the devotee's own energies unfold and are also drawn. Thus it represents the outer and inner spaces. Its purpose is to remove the object-subject dichotomy. In the process, the mandala is consecrated to a deity.

In its creation, a line materializes out of a dot. Other lines are drawn until they intersect, creating triangular geometrical patterns: the upright triangle stands for the masculine principle, and the inverted triangle, the feminine principle. The circle drawn around stands for the dynamic consciousness of the worshipper. The outlying square represents the physical world bound in four directions; and the lotus petals surrounding the circle represent the regenerative power and principles. The midmost or central area is the residence of the deity.

The entire mandala could represent a city, a palace or an island, but is most often the symbol of Mt. Meru, the mythical mountain made of solid gold and studded with jewels, the sacred triangle associated with the Mother Goddess. The human body could also be regarded as a mandala for, like Mt. Meru, it has a base and a peak linked by the spinal column – the column of Meru in which the chakras, energy centres, are located. It represents a powerhouse of energy.

The consecration of a mandala to a deity involves the inscription of Sanskrit syllables in appropriate places to transform them into energy or power representing the divinity. When a ritual is performed on the mandala, an effort is made by the worshipper to align his energy with that of the divinity, to activate the hidden external forces and the worshipper's own forces. In this ritual the consciousness of the devotee finds expression in articulation, it expands beyond subjective feelings and the external forces around, and there emerges spiritual development.

A Mandala in its usual or common religious context is a diagrammatic symbol of the object of worship. It can also be physical, not simply a diagrammatic design, but icons in human, quasi-human form — theriotheistic. It can be in animal form, or even aniconic objects, stones or crystals found in nature. It could also be symbolic artefacts like the lingam, or the discus of Vishnu, the trident of Shiva, or the spear of Devi. These are concrete and tangible representations of the deity; others, though tangible, are abstract with subtle curious mystical essence invested with meaning.

In ritual worship when icons are used, it is not unusual to draw the appropriate geometrical designs: the spirit of the icons is ritualistically invested in the design. In another yantra – the Surya Puja – sunrise or morning prayer – the diagram is drawn on the ground, which then becomes consecrated, a divine power site. An ordinary patch of ground or icon has to be transformed – cleansed – and the idol charged with the spirit of the deity. The mind of the worshipper must also be prepared by meditation for concentration, as it is his intention that makes the yantra a powerful instrument.

Yantra

This is a sacred mandala. The term has two aspects: 'Yan' means to regulate, and 'tra' to protect. Thus regulation is protection. It is therefore a device which regulates the energy dynamics of the worshipper, to protect it from decay, disintegration and death.

Before work on a yantra starts, the worshipper must meditate on its mystical form, for it is a sacred undertaking, to be able to invite or attract a particular deity to descend and endow the yantra with auspicious and protective power.

There are a variety of yantras, but the most sacred is the Sri Chakra, which could be made out of gold, silver and copper. The golden yantra is for worldly influence; the silver for health and long life; the copper for wealth. A yantra made of all these three metals secures all these aspirations.

A permanent yantra, fixed on the ground, is called *achana* – immovable. It could be an inscription on a stone, on metal plates, or carved on a rock. Once installed and consecrated it becomes a place of worship, an altar. A yantra that is not permanent must be reconsecrated to reendow it with power. There are also small yantras inscribed on pieces of crystals or metals, which are worn as charms. These are only given a sacred name; they are called dharana-yogya, fit to be worn on the body.

SRI YANTRA

The Sri Yantra is considered the supreme mystical mandala: it is also called Sri Chakra – the living yantra.

It is not prepared by an ordinary worshipper, but by a guru or teacher, for the work involved is an act of worship. He must be austere, must undertake fasting, seclude himself and meditate on the design for a period of time. It is not to be sold or bartered, but is usually given to a disciple.

The central power design must be carefully prepared. The square and the three concentric circles do not constitute the important integral part of the yantra, although they have their own relevant ritualistic symbolism.

The principal divinity of a yantra is the Mother Goddess seated in the central point – the Center of Bliss – represented by Shiva who, bereft of his own power, could not move. Devi is the life-giver, the inspiration. This is a Tantric discipline with the male-female symbol basic in the worship of the Sri Chakra. The female is superior; the male is subordinated to her.

The Goddess is dynamic; the God is inert; but they are inseparable: the Sri Yantra represents the two aspects. This union pervades the entire yantra but also endures in an unmanifested manner. The inseparability of the male and female principles is the important significance of the Sri Chakra.

The mantra of Sri Chakra is three-lettered. It is perhaps the three phenomena which caused the primary union of Shiva and Shakti, the transcendental principle; the initial emanation of the universe, its growth and harmony, and the absorption of the universe. The center of emanation is called Srishti-chakra, the center of preservation is Sthiti-chakra, and the absorption center is Sanhara-chakra. The first is presided over by the moon, soma, the second by the sun, surya, and the third by fire, agni. The triad called *tripura*, is fundamental and inseparable.

It is thus a psychocosmogram with a comprehensive overview of the entire process of creation. It has the principle or dynamics in its emanation, its beginning, its life, and its end, and the unmanifested power of resurgence.

Involved in the Sri Chakra is Kama-kala, the fundamental principle of all existence and experience. 'Kama' means desire, 'ka' means emanation, and 'la' absorption or the end. Thus, it means its desire, its emanation and its end. The first principle is desire, the primordial impulse, which produced the second principle, the emanation of light with a sibilant sound, which brought about the phenomenal universe. The third principle is its absorption or end.

The primordial surge (*spanda*) of desire was in the form of light (*prakasa*). This entered Shakti, the inspiration or transcendental essence, and produced the sound 'Aham' which means 'I' — the source of the experiential world. This is the OM mantra.

TRIANGLE

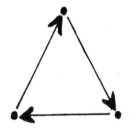

The kama-kala is represented by a triangle: one dot above, two dots below. The top dot stands for kama and the two dots for ka and la, or emanation and absorption, which are joined by a line – the fundamental base. The line which joins the top dot stands for emanation and the line which descends down to the other dot stands for withdrawal. It represents a unity of desire (point), the sound (nada), and the source (bija).

This upright triangle represents the male principle.

INVERTED TRIANGLE

The inverted triangle symbolizes the female sexual organ – the yoni. It has two dots above with one dot below; all three joined by lines. This is regarded as the basic form of the Mother Goddess. It represents the female principle.

This triangle appears more like the proper symbol of creation, with one dot at the bottom and two dots above. With one line from the bottom dot moving up towards the dot representing emanation, and then surging towards the dot representing withdrawal. It continues from there down to the original bottom dot – the source.

Mother Goddess

The Sri Chakra is made up of nine triangles, four upright, representing the male principle, and the five inverted triangles representing the female principle. The whole being represents a symbol of their union, it is the Mother Goddess that is worshipped in the Sri Chakra.

She is called *Tripura* because of her three forms: physical, subtle or verbal, and mental or transcendental. In the first form worship is external; in the second form by sacrifice, mantra or mental. The third worship is meditation; this is inner worship, as the human body is regarded as the temple of the Mother Goddess.

Ritual Worship

Obeisance is the symbolism of spiritualism. It is suffused with a profound belief in a Transcendental Being. It is worship in the mystery of human existence, which is repeated and becomes cyclical until it becomes a part of life. It is a human testimony of man's linkage with the Unknown.

Yoga Asanas

The asanas are ordinary physical exercises involving limbering and stretching with pranayama or breathing, and ending in poses or postures when breath is held or controlled for a period of time. This is known as khumbaka or breath control.

Central to the exercises is the maintenance of the human body in a healthy condition. There are Tantric asanas and postures which activate latent forces in the body. This is the kundalini — the Serpent Power — the female energy known as Shakti located at the bottom of the spinal column, which has to be aroused and stimulated to rise up to join Shiva, the male energy at the crown of the head.

Pranam

This is also known as *Namaskar*. This is symbolic obeisance to a deity, like genuflecting among the Christians, and also to individuals being in possession of the divine spirit. It involves the folding of the hands, palms together, and saying 'namaskar' on meeting or departing. It represents spiritualism, a form of worship, one of many in the social-religious-cultural life of the Hindu.

Surya Puja

This is the morning prayer, greetings to the sun. The worshippers, most often female, prepare their offerings of flowers, grains, water and a small lighted candle on a tray, and take it to their altars at home or out in the countryside.

The Hindu brahmins in Nepal prepare a yantra early in the morning on the ground during festivals in front of their housedoor or gate. They dye it with sindoor (vermillion with yellow and white powder) and place a few flowers and grains and utter a mantra to endow it with power.

It is also adorned with a center – the bindu or Center of Bliss — a representation of Mt. Meru. It is cleansing, drives away evil, and thus, it is a purifying as well as a protective sign.

III

NATURE'S MYSTICAL ELEMENTS

The physical consciousness of the environment brought an awareness of the munificence of nature which inspired the development of spiritual life. There took place enquiry into human nature which led to the discovery of the power within — the creative forces inherent in the human body.

Chandra

Chandra is the moon, a sacred element of nature, mystical in aspects. It is one of the *Tripura* in Tantra, the presiding divinity called *soma* in the initial emanation of the cosmos. This is an attribute of Shiva, Durga and Sambar. In its crescent form it is an ornament on the head of these deities.

Surya

Surya is the sun. It is the life-giving symbol and hence is the presiding divinity in the center of preservation of the universe. It is sacred and is worshipped.

Among the Hindus it is not the greatest; the greatest is the blue sky, the space, the Mother Goddess — on which it floats.

It is said that the real sun — the elan vital — is resident in the human heart. Its color is burnished gold and appears like a newly minted golden coin. This is what yogis or monks are striving with utmost effort to see. When it emerges, self-realization enlightenment is achieved.

Agni

Agni means flame. It is the first elemental force mentioned in the Rig Veda. In the early times of the Vedic Age, sacrifices were made to Agni, the fire-god.

It was originally employed as a weapon, but later it became a symbol of destruction, a precondition to the creation of a new life. In Tantra it is the divinity presiding over the center of absorption of the cosmos.

In ritual sacrifice it is an important offering. It represents the masculine energy, the fire-god, and is an attribute of Shiva, Durga and Kali.

Wheel

The wheel – chakra – round in shape implies rolling movement. Intrinsic in its shape are many potentials. It represents basically the sun, the full moon, the chakras and the lotus in the Hindu religious cultural landscape.

It represented also a weapon, like Krishna's discus, and later it became the symbol of life and death. As a ritual object it symbolizes a sharp instrument which severs obstacles in the attainment of enlightenment. It is an attribute of Vishnu and Surya.

The wheel with spokes in Hinduism does not represent the Dharmachakra. It implies motion – progress.

CHAKRA

The chakra is wheel-shaped; it is in Tantrism the center of energy and is whirling in motion. As a wheel it represents occult powers and symbolizes absolute completeness. It is associated with the practice of yoga, and Tantric meditation, for it is through the chakras located in the spinal column that the Shakti energy — the kundalini — rises stage by stage to join Shiva, the male energy, located at the crown of the head. It is an attribute of Durga, Vishnu and Surya.

FIVE ELEMENTS IN NATURE

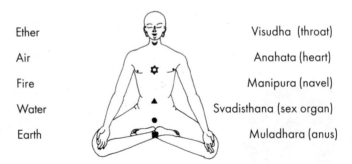

Ether	Visudha (throat)
Air	Anahata (heart)
Fire	Manipura (navel)
Water	Svadisthana (sex organ)
Earth	Muladhara (anus)

The five elements in nature are represented by chakras in the human body — the spinal column — chakras as energy centres are contact points between the psychic and the physical body. There are two other chakras; all together there are seven chakras.

Hinduism expounds the thesis that everything in the universe, including the tiniest atom, is interconnected. Centers of energy in the human body, represented as chakras, are not visible but their presence is apparently palpable.

They are represented as symbols, and in this introductory book are exhibited briefly as an essential part of Hinduism's mysticism. These symbols are necessary in the practice of *kundalini* yoga in Tantrism. This will be covered in another introductory book on the subject.

Besides the five chakras representing the five elements of nature, there are two other chakras which are very important, as they represent consciousness and the mind.

The Ajna chakra — the Third Eye — represents consciousness. In meditation this is one of the spots for concentration, in order to open it into full consciousness and to develop yogic vision, to be able to see the unseen.

The *sahasrara* chakra is on top of the head — the seat of the mind or pure consciousness. It is the seat of Shiva, the male principle. When Shakti joins Shiva here a transcendental mystical event is experienced.

This is the spot where the divine spark — the elan vital — when it rises up from the heart, finally settles. It disappears here. It is seen as glowing with a thousand lotus petals and is therefore brilliant.

This is what monks and yogis strive to see for self-realisation. It is to confirm by experience that this divine spark is in every living creature in nature.

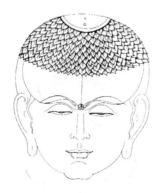

SWASTIKA

In Sanskrit it is Swasti. 'Su' means well; 'asti' means being. Thus it represents well-being or good fortune. Later, both in the Hindu and Buddhist tradition, it became the symbol of the Law. It also implies movement, time and life, and symbolizes the progress of the sun through the heavens and also sun-worship.

It is very old, pre-Vedic, indigenous to India and originally had mystical meaning. It is an abstract representation of metaphysical forces, of power, and is held with utmost reverence.

The right-hand or clockwise Swastika represents evolution; the left-hand or anticlockwise represents the winter sun.

It is an attribute of Brahma, Vishnu, Ganesh and Shakti.

PADMA

This is the name of the lotus. It grows in muddy swampy areas, but is a majestic plant which produces a beautiful flower. It therefore symbolizes the possibility of enlightenment even amidst difficult circumstances, where the impulse to struggle for salvation is strong.

Among the Tantrics it is the throne of the Mother Goddess; the symbol of the eternal font of mystic power, of beauty, joy and eternal renewal.

It is regarded as a sacred plant. Every part of it is significant: the stem represents the fact that all life springs up from water; the leaf the fertile earth; the bud virginity or purity; and the open flower the sun.

In Tantra it symbolizes the lotus-shaped chakras in the human body.

When the plant has petals both at the top and bottom end, it is called Visvapadmi or double-lotus. It is significant in that it reveals the importance of the deity who uses it as a pedestal.

It is an attribute of the Mother Goddess, Saraswati, goddess of the arts, music and literature, and of Lakshmi, the goddess of wealth and fortune.

The following simple geometrical figures are probably among the oldest non-Vedic indigenous conceptions of what they have observed as properties or qualities of the human body and of nature.

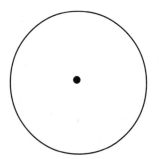

FEMALE PRINCIPLE

The circle with a dot in the middle originally represented the yoni — the female sexual organ.

This circle with a spot in the middle should not be mistaken for the symbol of the sun, which has also a blue or black dot in the middle. It is usually seen in this manner in the Third Eye when in a meditative state. This sun is seen like a moon because it has a white light with a dark spot.

This simple representation of the yoni, as shall be noted later, was revised: the circle was designed with a drainage outlet, with the black spot replaced by the lingam or phallus, the male principle.

YONI

This was designed later when it was discovered that the phallus was also in the anatomy of the yoni. The female sexual organ indeed as structured has a cleat — the phallus of Shiva. This is an important aspect of the female principle which the male principle does not have. Hence, the concept of the lingam-yoni: the lingam springing up out of the yoni.

It is for this reason that the lingam never stands alone by itself; it is always found set on a yoni. The two are inseparable. Together they represent union or oneness of the male and female energy. It is also a paradoxical symbol of both passiveness and dynamism. Both complement each other and the fundamental fact is that they can never be separated.

It is always Shiva, the lingam alone, that is often venerated or invoked, with the Mother Goddess completely overshadowed. In the indigenous lore and Tantra it is the Mother Goddess who is supreme. She represents the dynamic force, and Shiva, the passive state, is only one of the manifestations of her transcendental essence from which he emerged.

As a symbol of union, the lingam indeed appears to have sprung out of the yoni.

SHAKTI

Shakti is the name of the creative female principle. It is symbolized by the inverted triangle, which also represents the yoni. This inverted triangle represents the female energy known as Shakti, otherwise known in Tantric meditation as *kundalini*.

When meditation is successful, a mystical event occurs in the devotee of Shakti; suddenly this dark inverted triangle starts to descend upon the Third Eye. This is the symbol of Shakti.

As *kundalini* it is known as the Serpent Power, coiled three and a half times at the bottom of the spinal column. The purpose of yogic Tantric meditation is to arouse it to make it rise up through the different chakras until it joins Shiva, the male principle located at the top most chakra known as *sahasrara*.

When the *kundalini* is awakened, it sounds angry and it hisses like a serpent. The sibilant hiss continues until it reaches the *Sahasrara* chakra, and a mystical event takes place in the union of Shakti with Shiva. Self-realization is attained.

Shakti represents the kinetic aspect of the ultimate principle: the power that permeates all creation; it also means the consort of Shiva.

Male Principle

The evolution of the representation of the creative male principle came later, after the female principle, because of its power of transformation and reproduction:

 In its development the phallus evolved first;

 followed by the spearhead and

 then the mountain

 and the flame.

It became increasingly sophisticated, which indicates an ability to associate things of similar design or property or quality. They represent the male organ, male principle and male energy: the phallus or lingam – the sexual organ of Shiva. Also the spearhead, the mountain, the male principle and the flame the male energy.

LINGAM

This is the phallus of Shiva, the male principle. It is cylindrical, oval-shaped, an upright piece of rock in wild nature.

This is the most ubiquitous symbol of Shiva, 'the dark god of a dark people.' It is pre-Vedic. It is regarded not simply as a symbol of the male sexual organ or of fertility and reproduction, but it is also sacred as 'the essential shape of the deity himself, it does not merely imply, but directly expresses, the presence of the divine. It proclaims Shiva as the supreme force of the universe.

Apparently the lingam originally stood for the formlessness of nature, later for clear consciousness, and much later for Shiva, the masculine energy.

It is venerated often alone with a dash of sindoor — vermillion-yellow-white powder on top — the symbol of blood, an atavism of animal sacrifice practiced in earlier times. As a ritual object it is located in the sanctum sanctorum , accessible only by the truly devout or the priest.

Shiva-Shakti Yoga

This yoga means the union of the male principle, Shiva, and the female principle, Shakti.

It is represented by three symbols:

They are all abstract, but the abstraction moves from the simple to the complex: The first combines the original simple representation of the yoni — circle with the mountain as the phallus. The second represents two nuclei or energies, the male and female coming together. The third, a six-pointed star made up of two triangles, one inverted, the male and female principles.

All these symbols represent perfect union and enlightenment.

Six-pointed star diagram is also used in making an astrological chart.

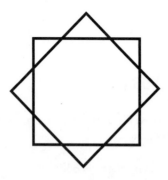

The eight-pointed star also has a mystical significance. This design is used in the preparation of a mandala, for apparently it is protective against evil spirits.

IV

DIVINE ANIMALS

In the evolution of Hindu worship, the auspicious aspects of the beasts of nature, their power and metaphysical qualities were employed as part of ritual artefacts. This bestowed power upon the deities, they became ornamental as their attributes and became their symbols.

In the world of dualism, made up of the good and evil, the deities were presented as theriotheistic, half-animal and half-human, possessed of destructive power in the fight against evil. They were given the beastly power of ferocity and brute strength. Only a few will be taken up as examples to illustrate the evolution of Hindu deities.

NAGA

Naga is the term for serpent. It is another universal symbol with metaphysical qualities. It is the only creature that represents a circle when asleep, but straightens up when awake. It either undulates or slithers in a zigzag motion. It represents a circle, the female principle; a phallus, the male principle, and when in motion the 'sperm.'

In Hinduism the snake is the symbol of the eternal cycle of time and immortality. It is worshipped as a divine or semi-divine being, regarded as a deity of the rain and guardian of the riches of the earth. Occasionally it is also regarded as a demonic being, which is also worshipped.

In southern India it is a symbol of fertility, and in the north a protective symbol. Vishnu as Panchanak has a canopy over his head made of five-headed serpent. Vishnu as Narayan (Vishnu Shesnag) sleeps on a bed of snakes.

Shiva, though, is the lord of serpents. The cobra is his emblem as well as that of Kali, his consort. In the Hindu kingdom of Nepal, however, it is not the cobra but the Naga Raja (King Snake), which is worshipped particularly during the Nagpanchami festival.

In Tantric discipline, the snake is regarded as a deity; it represents the mystical female energy and is known as Shakti. Coiled at the bottom of the spinal column it is known as *kundalini*.

Manasa is the serpent goddess. Her followers are called Nagas, those who practice Tantrism.

NAKULA

Nakula is the term for a mongoose. In Nepal, it is known as Naurimusa.

The mongoose is the arch enemy of the snake, but in ritual paintings they are presented together, the snake as guardian of wealth and the mongoose as the keeper.

It is associated with Kubera, the god of wealth, the counterpart of Lakshmi, the goddess of wealth. The mongoose is believed to be full of wealth, and when pressed by Kubera it gives forth riches of the earth.

MRIGA

Mriga is the name for the antelope. As a symbol it must be pre-Vedic. It became a symbol of the deities because of its attributes. It is powerful, agile and swift.

Like the skin of a tiger, which represents power, fearlessness and ferocity, the skin of the antelope became an artifact in ritual worship.

Shiva is occasionally depicted with an antelope on his left hand — a sign that he is the lord of nature.

MATSYA

The fish is said to be the first reincarnation of Vishnu, and is therefore associated with him as an attribute.

This is another creature which has a universal mystical significance. The *suvarna matsya,* a zodiac sign made up of two golden fishes, symbolizes good fortune and rescue from the misery of earthly existence.

V

DIVINE WEAPONS

In the evolutionary development of the Hindu deities beastly nature to fight evil was eventually discarded, and divinities began to acquire weapons. Divine weapons were endowed with mystical power and metaphysical significance.

The simple ones, made of wood, certainly must have predated the others. Some were made of human bones and skulls, which have esoteric significance, and others were made of metal.

TRISHUL

This divine weapon is an exact replica of the trident of Poseidon and Neptune, the former Greek and the latter, the Roman mythological sea-god. This one though is pre-Vedic, circa 3000 BC.

The three prongs denote the three attributes of God as creator-preserver-destroyer. The shaft represents the axis of the universe.

The trident of Shiva is called Sulla. Like the thunderbolt, it is regarded as a magic weapon that drives away demons. Like the cobra, it is an element of Shiva. It is also the weapon of Durga and is an attribute of Agni, the fire-god and Mahakala, the ferocious manifestation of Shiva.

SULLA

This is the divine spear, a weapon particularly of Skanda and Agni. Originally it was an invisible weapon of Vishvakarma, the creator of the universe.

GHANTA

This is a divine bell. It symbolizes the mystical primary sound — the origin of creation. In the hand of Durga, the Mother Goddess, it is a divine weapon, the sound of which inspires fear in the enemy. It is the characteristic attribute of Shiva and his wife, Kali.

It remains a ritual artefact, along with the conch shell, in Hindu worship.

VAJRA

This is a divine thunderbolt, the weapon of the sky-god, Indra. It represents nature's thunderbolt or diamond which destroys all kinds of ignorance, the quality of invincibility and invulnerability. It is in itself indestructible.

As a weapon of Indra, it was a double-edged dagger. It later became Shiva's 'Diamond Scepter'.

Vajra - Ghanta

The thunderbolt and the bell together do not constitute a weapon, but a divine instrument. In Tantric rituals the vajra, which stands for the male principle, is held in the right hand; the bell, which represents the female principle and prajna — wisdom, is held in the left hand. They are inseparable as ritual artifacts, and their interaction leads to enlightenment.

Parashu

This is the divine battle axe, the weapon of Parasuram, the sixth avatar of Vishnu, who descended to earth when summoned by the brahmins to fight the kshatriyas — the warrior tribes. The battle axe symbolizes the weapon which conquers darkness and ignorance. It liberates a man on the spiritual path from worldly ties.

It is also the weapon of the war-god, Skanda, but is also the characteristic attribute of Shiva and Ganesha.

KHADGA

This is the divine sword, a symbol of wisdom and enlightenment. It is a force of destruction, usually of worldly attachment and ignorance. As a ritual artefact it is worshipped and as a sign the longer it is the better. It brings good fortune.

KHETAKA

The khetaka is a shield. It wards off the attacks of the enemy. It is used by minor deities when their enemies possess demonic powers. A superior deity belonging to a higher order or who has an invincible weapon, never carries a shield. He does not need one.

DHANUSA - BANA

This is the divine bow and arrow. Alone, the bana or arrow, stands for the five human senses, and therefore symbolizes awareness. It is an attribute of Tantric deities, such as Marici, Kurukulla and Kama, the god of love.

Alone, the dhanusa or bow, usually carried on the left shoulder, is in itself a weapon. With it the god Marici punishes the Maras and other wicked beings.

Together as a symbol, the arrow stands for the male energy and the bow for the female energy. The arrow also represents the power of love, while the bow the death-wish. Together as a metaphysical symbol, they represent the balance between method and wisdom.

This was also the formidable weapon of Rama, the hero of the Ramayana epic, in his fight against Ravana.

CHURI

This is a dagger, used for stabbing. In religious rituals it symbolizes the sacrificial dagger. It is an attribute of deities in their terrifying manifestations, such as Durga and Kali.

KARTIKA

The kartika is a knife, mainly used for cutting or slicing. As a ritual object it represents the severance of worldly bonds. It is an attribute of Mahakala and of Dakinis, evil spirits who embrace the Dharmapalas, and also of the Yidams, such as Yama, the god of death and Yamantaka.

TARIKA

The Tarika is a chisel. As a ritual artefact it is comparable to the battle axe of Durga and Shiva. It has the same symbolic significance as the spear. It is the special attribute of Subrahmanya and Skanda.

ANKUSHA

This is a hook. The ordinary one is made of a wooden handle topped with a metal hook. It is called *ankusha* or *gada*, a goad used for prodding and controlling an elephant by the mahout.

The ritual hook is the symbol of action, the ability to distinguish the spiritual from the worldly motives. It steers one in the right direction and hence, it represents divine guidance.

It is an attribute of tantric deities, such as Ganesh and Skanda.

DANDA

The danda is a baton. The ritual danda is made of human bone also topped by a skull. It is used to punish offenders of the universal law of time. It is usually an attribute of deities in their terrifying destructive manifestations, like Durga.

GADA

The gada is a mace or a club, a weapon used in close combat. As a ritual artefact it is made of human bone, usually adorned with a skull at the top. This provides protection to the one carrying it and stands for the power of natural laws and of time, which destroys everything along its path.

As a club it is often depicted as a pestle and symbolically linked with the lingam and the staff.

It is the symbol of Vishnu, Shiva, Kali, Ganesh and Skanda. It is an attribute of Durga, Devi, and Bhairab.

VI

DIVINE SOUND INSTRUMENTS

There are really only a handful of sound instruments Most of them have been taken from nature itself, modified and improved upon by native technology. Others, with inspiration also from nature, have a more involved technology.

SANKHA

The sankha is a conch shell. In nature it is found on the sea coast for it is a product of the sea. In primitive times it must have been employed as a trumpet, like a bell, to gather the people for an important announcement.

In the Mahabharata — the Great Battle — it sounded the start of the war. It later became a ritual vessel in sacrificial worship.

The white one has a special humming sound, which is said to proclaim the glory of saints. Since its sound penetrates the atmosphere, it has become an attribute of deities, particularly of Vishnu.

The spiral in the interior of the conch shell signifies infinite space, which expands in a clockwise rotation. If its motion is anticlockwise the laws of nature are reversed. This type of sankha belongs to Shiva as the destroyer.

VEENA

It is a stringed musical instrument in India. It is the favorite of Saraswati, the goddess of learning, wisdom, the arts and literature.

Damaru

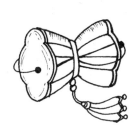

The damaru is a small double-drum with a leather thong tied in the middle of the drums. At the end is a piece of wood, bone or metal, which makes a rattling sound when turned swiftly, repeatedly upsidedown or from side to side.

Among the Tantrics the Damaru is made of two half skulls, which symbolizes the primal sound, the inception of the phenomenal universe, also the rhythm, vibration and strength of the cosmos. It remains a part of the paraphernalia used in ritual worship, along with the bell and the sankha.

It is an attribute of Shiva as Nataraj, the dancer, and is usually depicted along with the trident.

Flute

A musical wind instrument of Krishna, this is a symbol of an inner yearning, longing for the highest.

KANGLING

This is a trumpet, made of human thighbone. As a ritual artefact in tantric ceremony its sound is said to drive away evil spirits.

In combination with the damaru its sound becomes magical. It is used apparently during a celestial journey. Its music is regarded as being similar to a mantra in its power and effect.

VII

RITUAL ARTEFACTS & PARAPHERNALIA

The paraphernalia in ritual worship in Hinduism is numerous. Some items have universal application, like the beads and the book, others are very simple. They appear unlikely as religious artefacts, for example the lasso or noose. The rest are simply utensils essential to wandering ascetics, like their saffron robe.

Although nondescript and seemingly inconsequential, they symbolize a hidden meaning, always mystical. It is a significance that does not merely connote something potential, but something intrinsic and inherent in their nature.

Vanaspati

The mask is the symbol of Maya, the goddess of illusion. She is only another face of the Mother Goddess.

The mask has a mystical or metaphysical aspect or connotation. It presents the unreal, the illusory but hides reality — the transcendent essence of the divine.

The phenomenal world is illusory, beneath which is the invisible Primary Force. Everything is illusion. For this reason, there are numerous diverse masks. Also for the same reason, simple artefacts possess intrinsic meaning or significance.

It is a universal symbol, but in India the use of masks is pre-Vedic. It has indigenous origins, evolution and development. Its esoteric name is *vanaspati*, a personification of divine presence.

The *kirtimukha* is a mystical mask, which means the 'Face of Glory.' It has a grotesque demonic face, a magic design of protective character and is very similar to the Tibetan Bon-po mask used in their fire or demon ritual worship.

ROBE

The Hindu sadhu's robe is saffron-colored worn by the sadhus and sanyassins, the wandering spiritual mendicants, who keep moving from one temple to another, or to pilgrimage centers in their quest for knowledge of life and of God. The robe represents asceticism, renunciation of worldly existence and spirituality.

The sadhus or sanyassins do not live in monasteries, but depend for their subsistence on the hospitality and generosity of temples and people along the way. This tradition is found only in India.

The Nagas, followers of the tantric discipline and practices, do not wear any clothing, and are completely naked. They wear their hair long, and are covered with ashes from head to foot. Others of different disciplines or orders wear white robes, which represent purity.

RAKHI

This is a piece of string, a wristlet, tied by a sister or a woman on the wrist of a brother or a man, with whom she wishes to establish a fraternal relationship. On tying the wristlet a wish for long life for the would-be brother is made mentally. It establishes social responsibilities.

YAGYOPAVEET

This is the brahmanic cord made of cotton. The practice of wearing it is known in Hindu as Janeu. Between the age of twelve and twenty, a brahmin youth must undertake to put it on for the benefit of his parents. He must wear it before he can get married. It is therefore a kind of a rite of passage into manhood.

It entails an initiation ceremony. First he must bathe early in the morning, have a tilaka placed on his forehead and have his head shaved. This is followed by putting on the dhoti, a piece of saffron cloth known as *kundoni.* On completion of the rites he is now known as a brahmin.

In Nepal this is known as varthamanda; it is only for the Brahmin, Chettri and the Newari caste.

It is made of two pairs of threads each combined together to make the brahmin cord. Apparently the initiate is now considered twice-born.

PUSTAKA

Among the Hindus the *pustaka* refers to the Vedic volumes, the storehouse of spiritual knowledge. Thus it is the symbol of the mother's lap, or the lotus, or of wisdom. It is an attribute of Brahma, the creator, his wife, Saraswati, the goddess of learning, and Vishnu, the god-preserver of the phenomenal world.

DARPANA

     The *darpana* or mirror is a symbol of wisdom, but also of the emptiness of all worldly matters. It represents aspects of Shiva that are unmanifested. He carries it in his left hand as an attribute. It is the special attribute of Durga in her terrifying aspect.

SHIKHA

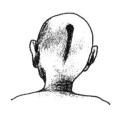

     This is the little tuft of hair on the shaven head of a male Hindu. It is also known as Bodi. On unshaven heads it is usually a little longer, it hangs out prominently. It sticks up in the center of the head and is regarded as sacred for it is the repository of spiritual energy. In tantra it is considered the point where the spirit enters at the time of initiation and the departure or exit point at the time of death.

     It is a protective symbol: because of its presence a Hindu can face any eventuality, including death.

TILAKA

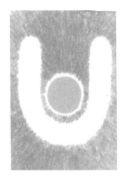

The tilaka in Sanskrit is the sacred dot. In Hindu it is called tika. When it is made of the ashes of cow-dung and it is called vibhuti, which symbolizes the transience of everything, including life.

This sacred dot is usually placed on the forehead, on the site of the Third Eye. It is placed there after the morning bath by uttering a mantra. It is a symbol of purification and protection. It represents a devotee of Vishnu, the god-preserver.

This is a practice which has not been taken up by the Buddhist.

Like the surya puja or the rakhi, the tilaka is often prepared by Hindu priests — usually for a small donation.

CHHATTRA

This is the parasol. Seen in portraits of Vedic gods and goddesses, it is a sign of royal power, and symbolizes protection, luck and happiness. It is the symbol of Vaikuntha, the paradise of Vishnu, and is the attribute of Ganesh and Vamana.

JAPA MALA

Japa Mala is the term for the mantra beads. It is a string of 108 beads, a number which has a special meaning both among the Hindus and the Buddhists.

The ordinary ones are made of wood, bones, pearls or crystals. The best ones are made of tulsi wood or the rudraksha seeds. Both the tulsi wood and the rudraksha seeds are medicinal.

They are not actually prayer beads, but are used for mantra. When used for this purpose, a mantra, such as Om or Ram, is articulated repeatedly over every bead. The completion of a round of 108 beads is called a *mala*.

It is an aid to meditation, as chanting a mantra leads to single-mindedness. It is held in the right hand. In chanting a mantra the beads are turned over only by the middle finger, with the index finger extended outward. Mental chanting is practiced, but it should be concentrated.

It represents the never-ending cycle or the eternal cycle of time. It is traditionally an attribute of Brahma, the creator and of Krishna, Ganesh and Saraswati.

SANKHA

The conch shell stands for the glory of holy men and absence of all evil. It is associated with Vishnu.

PRASAD

This is ritual food offering to the deities. It is made up of fruits on the whole, but sweets and cakes are also offered. In fact all sorts of food, including meat and the blood of sacrificial animals (still practiced in the Hindu kingdom of Nepal) constitute the basic offering. When the fruits, the sweets and meat have been blessed, the food is distributed around as *prasad*.

MAYURAPICCHA

Feathers are a symbol of immortality. The symbolic feathers represented are actually from the peacock and depicted as an ornament of deities, an attribute of their power. The peacock feather is an emblem of Shiva as Nataraj, the dancer. It is associated also with Krishna and Skanda, the warrior-god.

CHAMARA

This is made of yak hair, usually from the tail end and is ordinarily used as a fly-whisk. To the goddess Ganga it represents a weapon which drives away vermin. For Vishnu it is a royal sign and a lucky talisman.

It is the sign of a subordinate position of semi-divine beings and their attendants. It is also one of the eight symbols of good luck.

PASHA

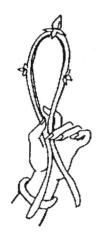

The pasha or lasso or noose symbolizes attachment to mundane matters; it also stands for the capacity of a god to capture evil and ignorance. It represents self-restraint. It is an attribute of Ganesh. It is found in the lower left hand of Ganesh.

SRUK

The sruk as a ritual object is a spoon used in religious ceremony to pour purified butter — ghee — on to the sacrificial fire. In the hands of deities it signifies that they also make sacrifices. It is an attribute of Brahma, Saraswati and Agni as well as Annapurna, a manifestation of Parvati.

SUKUNDA

The sukunda is an oil lamp. As a ritual artefact it is made of metal artistically designed with an image of Ganesh, whose presence is essential in the worship of the god as a bestower of success. In the lower part, the oil reservoir, there is a long wick which extends to the upper part, where its tip is lit during ritual sacrifice.

DIPA

This is a lamp which uses ghee, purified butter. As a ritual artefact it is considered sacred. During festivals and rituals, it is lit and offered to deities.

DHOOP DANI

This is an incense burner, either made of ceramics or metal. As a ritual object, incense is burnt as an offering to deities.

PADMA

This is the sacred water plant which represents mystical power, joy, beauty, purity and eternal renewal. It is an attribute of the Mother Goddess, Saraswati and Lakshmi.

BHIKSHAPATTRA

This is a begging bowl. In earlier times it was made of simple material, perhaps clay. As a ritual artefact its significance does not differ from that of a skull bowl and the sacrificial bowl or pattra. It is usually carried by wandering gods disguised as ascetics. It is an attribute of Shiva, Brahma, and Ganesh.

KAMANDALU

This is a water jug. As a ritual artefact it is a container into which the nectar is poured, but it also serves to pour it out. It is invested with a particular god or goddess of the devotee.

Ascetics usually carry it with them. It is an attribute of Brahma, Shiva, Varuna, Ganga and Saraswati.

SUVARNA MATSYA

Two golden fish together represent fecundity and salvation from earthly suffering. It is associated with Vishnu, the god-preserver.

KAPALA

This is a human skull, a symbol of life and death, of the impermanence of life and of things. It is a special attribute of Durga, Shiva and of Ganesha as Heruka.

HALF KAPALA

This kapala is the upper half of a human skull, which is often used in tantric rituals as a cup or bowl. When filled with blood it is called Asrkapala, and when filled with meat it is called Mansa kapala. The blood and meat are usually of a dead demon which deities feast on.

KALASA

This is a water jug believed to contain *amrit*, the elixir of immortality. It represents wisdom, immortality. It is placed on the altar as an important ritual artefact. It is also known as *khumba* or *kalasa*. It is an attribute of Shiva as a teacher, of Padmapani, the lotus-water goddess, and Lakshmi, the goddess of wealth.

CHATTRA

This is a parasol which represents highrank and protection against evil. ♪

DHWAJA

This is a banner which stands for a flaming lingam. In the hand of a deity it is a weapon. It is associated with Shiva.

SHIRIVASTA

This is an endless knot and represents luck, life and love.

DHARMACHAKRA

This is the Wheel of the Law. It has eight spokes representing completion and enlightenment.

PURNA KALASHA

This is a water vessel with all the eight auspicious signs. As a ritual object it is always placed in the middle of the altar, surrounded by eight smaller vessels.

VIII

A REALIZATION

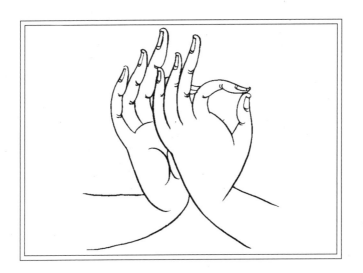

All the symbols are interrelated. They hold in them the basic philosophy, including the principles of the mystical aspects of Hinduism, which eventually bring basic knowledge of the composition of life and the universe. The quest culminates in the struggle to find the basic element in the human body — the spirit — the divine spark in the human heart.

In the end, after investing power in his own sacred symbols with the incantation of mantras in his worship of the divine, man finally realizes that the immanent power springs up from within himself.

He senses eventually that he is the one bestowing meaning and profound significance on his own creation — spiritual artefacts — in his search for reassurance in his earthly life from the Primary Force that gave form and substance to the phenomenal universe.

He discovers that the very essence he worships outside his being is actually within himself. It is the very essence that he bestows upon his own sacred artefacts. It is a reflection of his own nature of possessing the same mystical essence he endows his own ritual artefacts,

His own body, to his surprise, he discovers to be a temple of the divine spark.

What is left is for him to allow this essence to reveal itself in yogic meditation. It is a lonely struggle for no one can help him; he alone must undertake the ritual sacrifice in what is called the Inner Worship

IX

THE YOGI

The sadhu is a monk, who does not lead a monastic life. He lives in the active world and wanders like a sanyassin, who has left home, as a mendicant on a spiritual quest. He moves from one temple to another for a period of time, until he either settles in the forest, by a river bank, or in a cave to do prolonged meditation. This is inner worship.

It is a lonely quest. He must go it alone, for enlightenment or self-realization is experiential. He has to experience it in his own being. On this lonely route in life, in his spiritual quest he becomes a yogi.

A yogi is one who practices a certain path of yoga and who has attained a level of enlightenment, the outcome of discipline within a certain psychological and spiritual framework. A yogi is not alienated from life. His outer world is controlled by his inner life, firmly established within himself. All his thoughts and actions are to awaken his inner forces.

A yogi is the ultimate symbol of man in his own spiritual quest, finally taking recognition of his own potential inherent nature. He represents the Inner Worship in which sacred symbols have become unnecessary.

Inner worship is the highest form of spiritualism. Its significance is profound. It is yoga or union with the Absolute in a process which involves asceticism, self-abnegation, sacrifice or tapas, courage, fearlessness and great strength. Also unfathomable faith, quiet endurance of all sorts of privation, the attainment of the highest morality, and the crushing of the ego. It represents a cessation of the flow of the mind to allow the spirit to illuminate his being.

It is the symbol of enlightenment in which light in man has burst forth bringing in self-realization and a mystical blissful state in life. In spite of his detachment, his rejection of worldly life, he is joyous, for he has won the Absolute, the Ultimate, in his human experiential existence.

BIBLIOGRAPHY

Short Description of Gods, Goddesses, and Ritual Objects of Buddhism and Hinduism in Nepal, Jnan Bahadur Sakya, Handicraft Association of Nepal, Kathmandu, 1996;

The Book of Hindu Imagery, Eva Rudy Jansen, Binley Kok Publications, Diever, Holland, 1993;

Himalayan Pantheon, Daniel B. Haber, Book Faith India, Delhi, 1998;

The Science of Kryiya Yoga, Roy Eugene Davis, Taraporevala, Bombay, India, 1991;

From the Mating Dance to the Cosmic Dance, Swami Sivananda Radha, Sterling. Paperback, Delhi, 1992;

The Wheel of Sharp Weapons, Dharmanaksita, Library of Tibetan Works & Archives, Dharamsala, 1976;

A Beginner's Guide to Krsna Consciousness, Bhakti Vikara Swami, Shaktivedanta Book Trust, Bombay, 1994;

Hindu Mysticism, S.N. Gupta, Motilal Banarsi Das Publishers, Delhi, 1992;

Agnihotra, Swami Satya Prakash Saraswati, Swami Satya Pratisthana, Lakhimpur-Khur, Allahabad, India, 1985;

Sri Chakra, S.K. Pamachandra Rao, Sri Satguru Publications, Delhi, 1989;

Folk Origins of Indian Art, Curt Maury, Columbia University Press & Oxford-IBH Publishing Co., Calcutta, 1969;

The Yoga of Love, M.P. Pandit, Lotus Light Publications, Wilmot, Wisconsin, USA, 1982;

Sri Lalita Sahasranama, Swami Tapasyananda, Sri Ramakrishna Math, Madras, 1993;

Kindle Life, Swami Chinmayananda, Central Chinmaya Mission Trust, Bombay, India, 1996;

Sacred Hindu Symbols, Gautam Chatterjee, Abhinan Publications, New Delhi, 1996;

Other Titles in This Series
by Book Faith India

For Catalog and more information Mail or Fax to:

PILGRIMS BOOK HOUSE
Mail Order, P.O.Box 3872, Kathmandu, Nepal
Fax: 977-1-424943
e-mail: mail@pilgrims.wlink.com.np
website : www.pilgrimsbooks.com